Coat Of Arms

Coat Of Arms

Chris Tysh

Drawings by Catherine Tirr

STATION HILL

Published by Station Hill Literary Editions, a project of the Institute for Publishing Arts, Inc., a not-for-profit, tax-exempt organization, Barrytown, New York 12507.

Grateful acknowledgment is due to Wayne State University, the New York State Council on the Arts, and the National Endowment for the Arts, a Federal Agency in Washington, D.C., for partial financial support of this project.

The author wishes to thank the Michigan Council for the Arts for a grant which helped in the writing of this book. Her special thanks go to Dirk Bakker, Lesley Brill, Jerry Herron, and Eric Wheeler.

Cover design by Susan Quasha.
Typesetting by Dorinda DeLiso.

Drawings by Catherine Tirr, used by permission of the artist, copyright © 1992 by Catherine Tirr.

The quotation on the dedication page is by Richard Klein from "In the Body of the Mother," *Enclitic*, 7 (1983).

These poems have appeared in *Big Allis, Bombay Gin, Everyday Life, Mirage, New American Writing, O•blek, River Styx, Southpaw* and *Triage.* To all editors, grateful acknowledgment is made.

Distributed by The Talman Company, 131 Spring Street, New York, New York, 10012.

Library of Congress Cataloging-in-Publication Data

Tysh, Chris
        Coat of Arms / by Chris Tysh.
                    p.   cm.
        ISBN 0-88268-111-7
        I. Title.
        PS3570.Y65C63   1992
        811'.54--dc20   92-16318
                                                                 CIP

Table Of Contents

because
"the father is the father insofar as he is not, is the
absent father—always already dead."
to my mother, my love

Coat Of Arms

O, to przetarcie sie bielma, o ta inwazja blasku,
o, bloga wiosno, o, ojcze…

Oh, that shedding of the film, oh, that invasion
of brightness, that blissful spring, oh, Father…

—Bruno Schulz

Finally there were various plastics easily influenced kitchen.
That is to say walking along a corridor diapered in vert
borders a carpet like early fainting, maybe an Italian boy
with violent fondness for eggs, a sort of punishment one found
necessary those days of vested falls, certain it was trippant
to simply use a bucket with a goutté of piss.

Some, having little talent for composition slept on the stairway
in reference to a country, strapped omnibus, lavaliere, not seen
again. In other stories admittedly intolerable much happens
short of tender and gold. Indeed was a piano, ideological
furs to comb.

Early examples are waisted, inviting enough light and humor
likely to form a powdered field of bars-gemelles.
"Her dad went off to war" some would say it like that
without severity, a long aching falling from the shoulder.
They had only to hold in hand a wallet a coat to be vastly
in arms. The use of azure suddenly lost in the herald's paint box.
One starts with heart's tincture per cross on a burning
hill, pierced by a silver thing or such closeness there are
chequy regularities in the marshalling of these ceremonies.
A way to see the major's widow cuffed with ermine
although not wealthy, forty-four recently and a child
at home. All the waving music, tall tea left unfinished.

Everyone has got a coat a bed a breakfast in the course
of winter when it is lined with windows of propaganda.
Known gradually as current securities to grow hair like
flowers, skipping in bend such as corn until sunday husked,
it does mark a change one feels contemplating so much or,
asleep in uniform under bedding partly clear of speech.
Has everyone got a painted bath to follow the flag with,
arm raised in salute holding a feather a crystal or what-
ever occurred, signifying : It's a pleasure to be placed
here: causing lather around the face, later on floor
what remains, the lesson, is a stain. There could be
nothing more apparent in the quality sold as mirror.

Ce qu'on appelle corps is a field.
Anything, almost anything can be placed on the field.
A breakfast tray invected for convenience is going to seem
hot and more susceptible of error than the handsome right
to bear arms of thought voided between two windows azure.
But what shall be said of the bed which is fortune
upright and a passion ever so singular it slips quarterly,
always white linen cut away to show pale throat paler
through the opening as if blaming air, cool admitted.
That metal shall not lie on metal makes choosing plain
mirror, crumbs around it she begins to fold here & there
angles, "memory," the hourly wage addressed to her story.
Certainly it has reached that moment when someone falls dead
in the center, semy with birthmarks and pasturing stock.

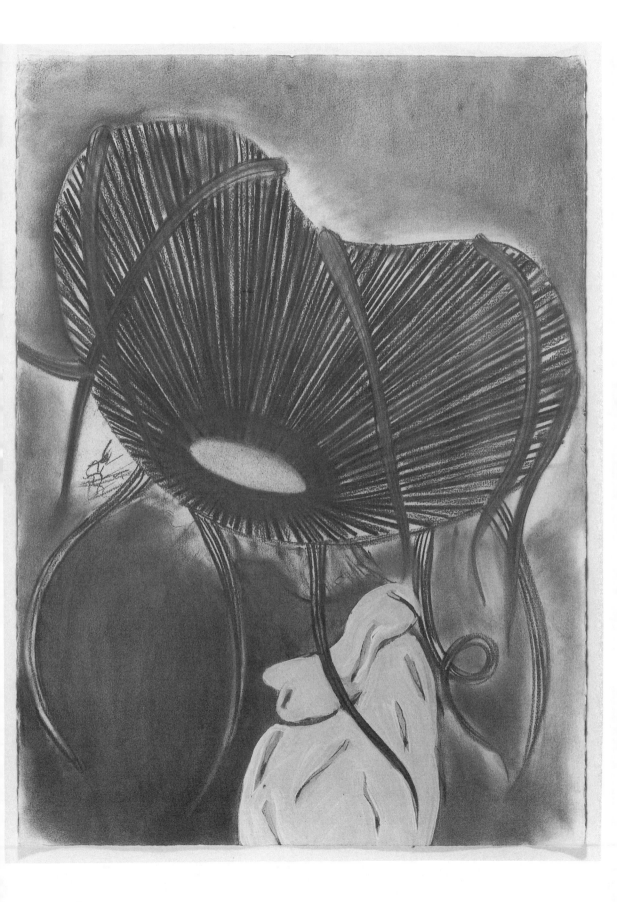

Books had always been carried in suitcases. The widow
kept money in *PALE FIRE*. Big denominations with silver
and red quarters stationed for months under cover of
brains. The smell of butter roux. She could never
remember the recipe. An event is told earlier than others
anterior to it. Whole years passed in silence is tight
fitting. A tropism for falling in crowded places. More
squarely a room with red floor in it. These books are
necessary the child is saying to himself which is
window. It shows a light rain pelting the plush velvet
field. A single grenade must be delivered. There seems
little doubt a cap of maintenance follows the arrangement
mentioned in passing. How readily the weeping pulls
into march.

"As a soldier it is my duty to hide." With an eye to
climbing, fear of wet, how it slips, adopts, invents a
son or daughter may wish to view the habit of carrying
his name with circumspection. To know how and under
what roofs, hands pull, do they happen for a reason,
one speaks the way he does. Was the female entourage
mistaken. A little rouge & desperate in conversation.
Per pale argent and sable five red stars stand sure
on a chest others depict as flattering. Errors do
exist. Of course there will be no chattel in bed.
Increased hazards betray marital status or such
portion of the letter facing bread or even sweet-
meats boxed at the trenches like, "you have no idea
what tastes I had then."

That anyone should have imagined the existence of a day-
bed azure fretty on the continent with the inevitable lace
iron to provoke a perfectly reckless exchange could only
have the slightest foundation in fact comes pink to nothing.
"I like to think, little girl, I tried, *ma vierge folle*,
to calm my blood but it was not for me." Pleasant little
insanity weighs less when teased into a ball. A fragile
dog would be awkward considering the crop of rumors held
by the cushions, all sable, flag and pennants. Nervousness
does come followed by deep crystal ashtray suggesting
argument. On such occasions a skirt, navy-blue is speech
best seen rushing in front and pleated. Woof. Hot water.
Ankles. Nothing will have taken place except a brush with
tearing. In the future satin slippers are found under
the bridge staging further hostilities, greener curtains.

Once adopted a figure of speech demands residence
in those labors. Remembering common charges opens a wall
of complications, like faulty scaffolding upon her
marriage. A sharper slope makes fusily. That is severe
heat and emigration. She and someone else with her
allow each other's temporary coats to disappear in favor
of a little rash. Paper identification pressed into
service. Will they dress up for the occasion in seamed
stockings and jealousy. It begins as follows: skipping
some words containing u's she is worked and waves.
All through summer he cries freely though he cannot admit
partings in the field are ordinaries: a sinister half
shading and discretion.

What was the use of all these interdictions: sour milk,
denim, wheat ears in the quotidian drapery of a household.
Paraphrasing described as mulish becomes water carrying
the same number of objects which flow without difference,
so thin it is a kind of roundel, modern tendency for
orphan. Shock margin, their hands stagger to look like
terracing poor land. Facts form tents for defeated soldiers
by the light of war. Supposedly this sitting and speaking
has a special status, granting the reader immediate possession,
folding table placed against logic, barely absent from its own
clutch and clatter. All he had wanted, make it every male,
spiked or dawning, arches over a single paragraph. *The station-
master's wife in her garden.*

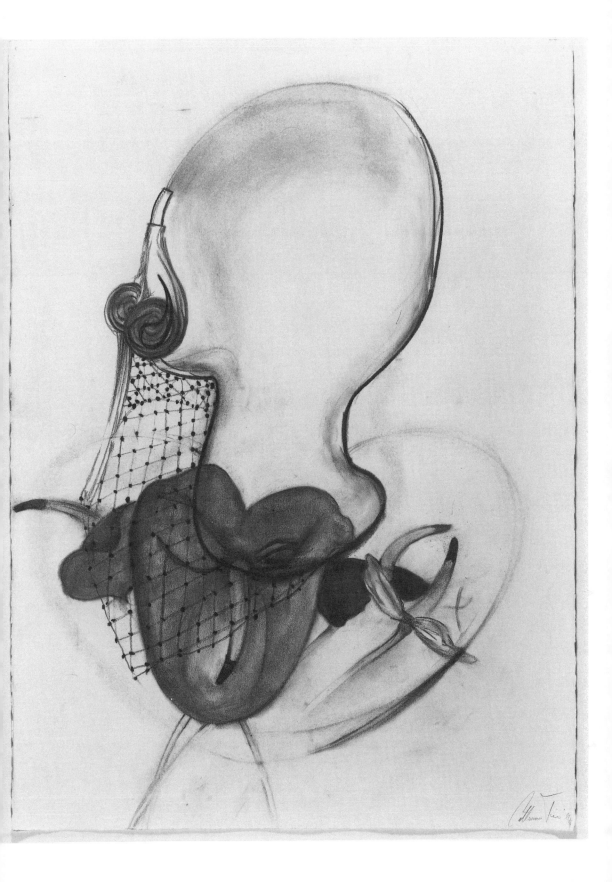

"They've questioned me again." *Es kommt nicht so sehr darauf an, das die Luft* yes the air, including sleep will have to duck, fenced in the night apparatus of prejudice. Hands generally couped at the wrist appear incarnadine, everything missed, flashing. The man is simply looking past his shoulder, he is regardant. Should he crouch now, not quiet her, mouth fastened with crimson, sink his chin in the emotive flora, he marks a spot younger growing toward the street. Should he then decide, if satisfied that all is well, purple stem and leaves piled up high, to proceed, he may want to retard, swollen with a tenacious need for shouting, the twin thrashing of the hour.

Unwillingly the arms of a woman when so many weaken
will raise an army (money revolt a building) her voice
actually her children will remember a vanity opera with
large types running for reasons of sentiment or policy
in open coats it will be april between clouds of cloves
everyone will shout PRIMA APRILIS at the appointed moment
buckets of water will drown the flimsy footings of the
next generation. When seen from that standpoint or away
from it, the object of such solicitude will appear adulterous
later red and silver mantling and sewing a strap on a
recondite turmoil. Won't the night bring something punitive
to the air they breathe, the bark agreed upon.

Woof and warp. Yes a radio. No adjectives bring.
Food local medicine. After independence a. Form of crude.
Love affairs consuming. This already abbreviated. Scene
outside Belleville. If a woman. Has no brothers. Her
beauty is. Skin cushioned by. Memory claiming passage.
On heraldic waters. Not a swan. Argent on bend. Gorged
with coronet. Hammer and sickle. Drooling picayune stir-
rups. Anyone can learn. To bend knee. Throw a shadow.
Ferdinand de Saussure. Died in 1913. Supporters because like.
Spelling it produces. Factory a bruise. Think of how.
She knew desire. At 15 in. Her mother's dress. The
delirious shoes. Worn against identity. The night porter.
This craze for. Meaning cuts sleep. Make vagaries of.
This reality one. Is not sure. There is hesitation.
When the person. To whom the. Mailman speaks recognizes.
Herself in that. Speech at home. In a boarding. School
she sees. Instruments placed on. The wrong side. More
or less. A theater bore. Strip-tease of. Dreams serious
disease. Sensitive to signs. A white villa.

and in the moments of oblivion when mouth
and leg draw profit upon a chair the idea
of terror tied to music (a mess in his hands)
moves closer to intelligence. Such is the corset
of will, sheriff bindings at work like aorist
verbal structures pressing, conducting bar
and the day seems longer increasing the cost of
narration beyond necessity. Already one is nourishing
(fag end last pastry puff) a dead notion, mauve
around the waist, a hunter's hound drawn with
drooping ears. She will have to, in her compliment,
erase what is wanting, blue and rose in the middle
candy cotton is a pretext, a short courtship
of a building: her "own room" to study ill in.

you obtain an assignation with the heiress.
Rather than going mad you run the last few years
over again into morning bands like exaggerated
awnings one sees in certain quarters. Whether
the blazon mentions it or not there are leathers
held in sleep, red trousers after each palm.
Such scoldings in the curtained bed, you may
tell yourself: so much depends on what goes white
in the painting, this habit of the artist for
palimpsest, to say nothing about the damaged
dress, blind hand and wishing. You are beginning
to find the alleged metaphor a little tarnished,
something to do with ancient mirrors. Beauty
abounds on the agenda before your mind comes
apart, your hair intact in its summer fan.

ARMIGER WHO WILL SAY SPASIBA panorama tutu riot for me.
Who can seize the sentence of his ancestors, husband
the oval goods, jejune tracings of skulls and hearts
vambraced beyond baroque. Must I remember how I got
here so many windows to gladden, reeds, even grass
arrogance appear in patches. Sooner hatless and dog
rose on blood or dirt between sleepy officers the room
itself abandons logic, cheap linoleum inside a story.
What is intended as flashes of apparent grammar, links
fesswise, the one with the regime. Applause sheets
acquired in broad twine, these tourniquets from above,
hanging in century's youth. Could she, if fitted
with color, lie in this paragraph, a slight torsion
in the writing, like, *dear mama*, I have little latin
or pedal to pull rank now, stuff mouth with dressing
when everything summers in water and returns at night's
end canceled to folly.

we were always having to read the rubato version of things

very far afield a dialogue strikes the branches
of a mourning family. Below this sentence a widening
thunder, orchard, fiction. (March 5, 1957.) On the
outskirts of sleep, it's understandable, her migraine
invades the text we hold pressed to our side, although
not bound by the intelligence of others. Opening the
door to fear, we are gradually swamped, splattered with
a sense of injury, yellow coats, unfigurable against
the world, not to be mended soon. From the beginning
that strange disposition of character, same absence
about the eyes, random longings painted on the mouth
substitute for events anterior to language. A widow out,
offers (no) resistance inside cloth, spreading like
pronominal poppies that furor should salute at this
moment of her thinking and falling into ruin between
two storms

Per pale azure and sable, two hubbies in chief proper
and in base a wave running to wood.

Azure: in each, a bed nebuly and slashing between
as many propositions or.

Gules, on a plain bend her hair pendant from its ribbon,
couped at the neck.

Or, and for distinction, a slip charged with mirrors,
all in pretence.

Out of cloud, turned up ermine, a cavalcade.

upon death her arms are removed no control is exercised over the wording

                    to perceive the marks of degradation
mock the grotesque braggadocio interchangeable with butter
money into pastries like paintings the potlatch of women
to be in highly controlled circumstances all alone the basis
for representation, say eminently quotable body, the syntax,
each sentence narrowing down the possibilities, how property,
ownership, etc. doesn't mean foreigners, member for class,
anything with male issue, himself a peer whose pleasure
is drawn in excess all these years like violent femmes
sweeping by
                    to exile, obstruct, interfere with a generation
of meaning: her breasts formerly little milk statues you'd
give up music with the signature in sharps, theme of separation,
in the middle she took no precaution, for instance fruit
trees, ruse, yellow brick road to the far end of infinitive
construction, what's crammed onto the descriptive table,
a few nagging platitudes having to do with understudies
in a cabaret, charged with three bombs a ruined monument

                    to be at loss for divertissement postpone
grievance, eye collyrium with the intention to balkanize
obstinate notions, make sharp lies in the mass of land,
it would unfold in the album, same color as written piazza,
now brushed aside in the fray, that squat laughter

Some events have no observable contours, twice the neck
to the small extent that inanimate objects are found lacking
there is some feeling, lighted torches and footing cavalierly
depicted in the absence of mirror we exhibit ancient manners
already subject to dispersion, easy pin traffic. One could've
said bastard language dragged across the loft, belly method
a schoolgirl in uniform falls straight back to the house
genre of illusion, that *mahlerishe Figur* rampant in this way
over everything in which she is contained, a series of photo-
graphs rather than torrential mechanism of affection, we know
the gallant fictions at the end of the eighteenth century,
always broad understandings structured like hands on the side
of raiment, grassy garters tied to continental leisure, those
with last trace of delirium he lays flat in the corridor,
counting. What they see talking to each other is erased
at thigh, pearls on spikes across the screen: band of hooks,
phantasmatic lashes. Few commission such views.

n'a pas de direction, à peine une sorte de terreur

vers la mer, cette possibilité vêtue de phrases clandestines

désigne une attente, un lieu-dit comme une corniche

ou femme au sommeil pauvre, bouche ivre il lui arrive

de saisir une violence, envie d'abriter à elle seule

les formes interdites d'un discours qui la sépare

des autres. L'éventail est largement ouvert, SLASHING

BETWEEN AS MANY PROPOSITIONS OR. ON A PLAIN BEND

HER HAIR. Minuit panache d'un récit obscène, COLLARED

& LEASHED on y promène celle qui compose l'objet caché

de notre angoisse. Ses longues jambes nues, légèrement

pliées, elle (persiennes, l'appartement de X, magistrale

guêpière-fiction) tarde, fait durer le texte qui s'ouvre

à cet endroit à la blancheur mécanique du non-dit.

Napa deer wreck scion, open-sorted terror
Vermeer settee, vested possibility of clandestine phrases
designs a tent, only did come cornice or femme
o' some poor butch ivy Louis, are riveted.
Say sire a violence, envied arbiter ails soul
lest forms interdict, deign a discourse-key, less
pared otters. Leviathan east, largely meant oeuvre,
SLASHING BETWEEN AS MANY PROPOSITIONS OR. ON A PLAIN
BEND HER HAIR. Minute pan ash duns, recites obscene
COLLARED & LEASHED any pro men sell key, compose,
lob jet, cashed neuter angst. Say long jambs knew,
ledger mint pliés, ale (persian, X's apartment, magistral
Gay-Pierre fiction) tardy fête during the text's key
over a set android, all blanch hour, mechanic dew, none dit.

"It turns out I was terribly wrong, followed
to the eldest son, perhaps even his face who
has inherited the troping grey eyes, older marks
of forensic embellishment, by ape supporters, flanking
day-trippers in raised ladders as if such flattery
obtained the very heart of the subject: a little
black carriage of mourners on display, three of them
touching while a grassy mound is skirted, closer
details in every direction. A divorce takes place
as part of a complicated system of representation,
biscuit twins spoon panic, stabbing the ground,
all clamoring through the scarlet imaginings, it
could be a common practice, no longer the high-ceiling
charm reserved for theater. How *did* things happen,
the shaft of a boy may taper to a point I break
and traffic with the souvenir of a smile, that
which insinuates, performs, writes. Incredibly fake."

dear reader, allow me (je ne fais que passer) palazzo
shoulders, fictive drafts. There are no guarantees we shall
come to shore in the absence of an original speaker, like
a school of rowing toddlers in drag and necklace we favor
last minute rescue, anything importing the maternal presence,
even most remote phantom of likeness will do, a mere trace
of jersey acquiesce, will identify a cemetery up on a hill,
its strawberry leaves pursued. What was the use of all these
interdictions: sour milk, denim, wheat ears in the quotidian
drapery of household? Could I commute my obligations, once
again splash the lingering lingerie with suspect rhetoric,
the train of my disappearance. A concertina wire in its barb
raises the question of infinite regress, small forgotten
repetitions dog the penchant avenue. Cushioned by the window
you can't tell what marks a fall at such late hour. It boils
down to a sunken inscription spelled with the disreputable
grammar of cartoons, orange carousel subject to ruin. There
lies the unattended pavilion of reading.

armorial   bar   cockatrice   diaper   ermine
fretty   grant   heiress   inverted   jessant-de-lis
knot   latticed   mantling   nebuly   or   pale
quarterly   roundel   sable   tincture   urchin
vambraced   women   yale   zodiac

achievement   bend   cock   delta   expanded
feather   graft   hand   impaling   jambe
key   lodged   marshalling   night-ape   ondoyant
parted   queen's coat   reversed   sun-in-his-splendor
trussing   unicorn's head   vair   wreath of laurel

that name?

wrecks everything, mother made it up under interrogation

her repertoire?

basic greek, furnish the story with incendiary emotions,

elevate X to Y

the suitcases?

books. The widow kept money in *PALE FIRE*

hysteric?

by all accounts. This image is accommodated in a sentence:

"Her pain is demonstrative, like a rose slipped and leaved."

in the thread?

the prolonged maintenance of sexual fantasies, family

jewels deserving her tenderest ministration

could it be…?

no sooner had she grasped the parts than she was pressing

further into the whole foreign substance with a striking

lack of modesty

and then?

turning the pages the arrival of war: fragment, deconstruction

limit her *violon d'Ingres*, lighter sketches rub out

The French window will not open to the charge of frivolity,
anonymous stains and the proposed series of citations
only intended to slip and dodge the more difficult task
of duplicating what gradually ceased to exist. Half-raised
to the illusion of climax, it draws its relation from
the indecent exposure of the observer, heavy red bands
move into the frame getting an easy purchase on the enigma.
Pending defenestration, even inanimate objects acquire
narrative status, shed tears on account of heroine, as if
this mimicry alone could undress the sumptuous body accredited
by the golden triangle. The latter must be drawn on wood,
become crest or gripped in a mailed fist.

In reserve, in the vicinity of an unmade bed, the narrow
colophon of realism gives permission to a theme. A
solitary cock throws up at the mouth.

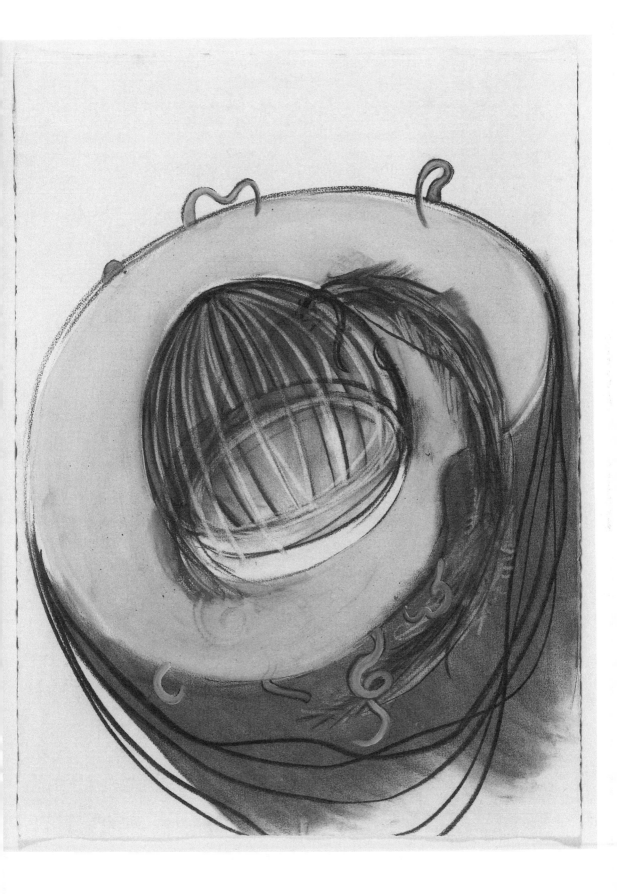

In the slanted portrait of these divestments one recognizes
a change in color reaching down to the tips drawn with ex-
cessive, gauze-like manner, as if barely allowed upon the
subject, to raise familiar initials, much less construct
a first-person narrative tied to a very young girl in flaring
skirt. Under such circumstances there isn't much concern
for cutting hair on a line parallel with reverence to weather-
cock, the longer evenings of prosperity, her lips and nipples
the obligatory shades of madder she is suspected of making
up under strict control. Despite the risky practice of
depressing the original contents (last pastry puff a mess
in his hands), one proceeds with what is left of the bordure:
so faint a strip it becomes nebuly, teasing out the violent,
inadmissible parade of "a objects," i.e. pipi, caca, lolo, etc.

unless of course it is supposed they were sneaking away
from behind the classical camera lucida, its overarching
garden formulas like some preposterous confession on a death-
bed chaperoning their desire, mirror and latch, to bolt out
of sequence, disremember the blushing accents upon a chief;
the weeping image both precedes and survives all versions,
need not be inconvenient reference to fever, tiresome furniture
in the child's mouth, rather some pneumatic envoi to crowd
the escutcheon with crated letters, she can become *air, this
hollow* if her father dies in a state of lexical suspension
which leaves the communiqué intact while a curtain rises on
the Officers of the Realm speaking without detours nor much
fear of interruption about simple devices they paint in vivid
colors, notwithstanding the syntax of the new sanctions
(these should be repealed), the first maintains upon an inter-
minable sentence, the recollection of her mother, all normal
positions for a brisure put into traffic at once

more plausible than others advanced in the past
the manifest contents of a slip. their very
slimness presupposes an ordinary fabric, most
likely a blend of cotton-wool and abusive duties.
perhaps this was an odd excuse, dyed blood-red
until recently but kept nonetheless for what it
concealed in italic readiness of the more vintage
stuff, a leash so made there are strangers
who pass by. (between cup and lip.) some
guarded use of anteriority may attend the masked
ball in full swing, roll down its hair so to speak,
against evenly troubled nurseries. almost like
a proper name the material goes public overnight
with its tendentious identity, counterfeit panels
tilting on the way to the bedroom. the idea of
including portrait sleeves, veils, bands of fur
only exaggerates the doctrinal fainting of women,
how they slip and slide across the corridor
toward the invisible scalloped edges of perversion.
shades of empire can be detected in coffee, famous
gaffe.

So too the autarky of love. At the piano
besides a chaise longue a belief which sustains
in the last resort healthy suspicions, the fort/da
traffic of immoral trinkets, that portion of bread
left on the oilcloth after dinner, if any
hardness of flesh lies in the way it corrupts
the questioning glance. Long after the means
of distinguishing a man from his vocabulary
have faded, a shooting colt is heard, transom
flood. Rotary presses deepening in on a wall
snatch fingers, tie bottles, the veins in a leaf
over leg of powdered continent. And plumbing
veneer stares. Gruel as through a window
trembles in the sluttish spoon. A coat already
quartered fills with water, just hangs there
like a dented linchpin inside her bra.

They go in pairs. All manner of baskets
sporting flirtiest bandage   red spanking box
rupture the cardboard mounting of this
come-hither scene. Unrecorded pistol days
on the continent, as yet non-private vehicles
there could be smaller favors, so jealous of pain,
exclamation points you squeeze into a heart-shaped bustier
of expletives:

                eyelet holes
                or any endless rhetorical loop
                fringed with gold garters

                            begging for buns
as it were, the apparent voice of a narrator
fetter, trees, wide straw hats, silver gilt balls
                returns us to dress and suspect charm
of guilty parties. Let's be unconscious
someone moved following loss of previous royalties
three escallops, a gray mullet, fudge
apologies. To enlist the mirror stage, sooner or later
these kissy hands   a word is wanted   close enough to fuse
those moments together
one could've said bastard language dragged across a loft,
belly method in the captive text

More than a little crenelated for defense
the figure of the absent father, even book
covers are stamped with it.

If tongue be a woman's arms...
　　　　　　　—Laura Moriarty

with these specifications in mind (faggoting
detail drawstring bottoms) I hold the chair,
obtain various nails, bows to sinister. It
will just have to balance on its central self-
admitted femininity, long hanging frame among
the amusements of the period. Although this front
elevation is normal and toolproof our castle
is like a round tower we know better than
to stand outside when buckles appear on straps,
neither thrashing nor yellow. A little shepherd's
pipe, the tongue should hang down, many hanks
of cotton palmed off on simulacrum's peacock
status. Some harder knocking might be asking
for violent dispute instead of merely decorated
redness banded in light and dark gray shadows.
Sometimes dropped by a lady, a key has its
wards, a ring finger its violin, rummaging

truth is a widow
—Norma Cole

that a soldier's black and untasselled
makes the writing seem demure, out of sync
with nakedness of his face, mounting probability
pressed into the couch as I watch him
from my way station for boarding & refreshments.
Back home, the reader will remember to insert
a hatchment, for instance before extinguishing
lights, whimsical strings in the filigree
of paternal chronicles. Under the umbrella
of experience, intense and binding *klangfarben
melodie*, my hospitable apron prefigures
the foreign recitation of a wet dream.

crude though they were a man and his class
bid us review the crowded buffet, deep
cleavage in the word *acumen*. We consent to wet
issues, portico salad days following sampling.
A greenness we were to lose in yellow spencer,
balmacaan, hottest pink tube skirts of falsetto
train. In a broad sense the point of departure
is always on top these vamps, pin-ups jump
the adored queue before jersey factories open.
The head is now speaking from a balcony.
Comparison breaks down, weighs the music rack
with *Everything Happens To Me*. If proportions
be grouped, become preface for occupying the bar
and chevron. Canvas sexual wreck. Brides lecture
husbands in neglect and customary signs of affection.
Any other sentence—amaurotic breasts—is a plot.

after hearing depositions the jury adjusts.
Two sets of truth are better then. One doubts
clemency of weather, any dark eyes fringe
diaspora tulle. Touted detail escapes panopticon
reading filmed at close range. Or else we must can
one dub, too dull later rolls, already designated
lack. What occasions death grew between them,
might apply there on the bottom, instanter. "Blue
eyes, white skin" narrator's on the dole, she
will gladly bracelet tutor surplus stock immediately
hung over, one of them said to be a retainer, i.e.
holding a letter set full face grille as if trying to kill
two birds without. On a net habit, beret of shade
she's engaged, each follower of Thot in same slap
dash pushcart with five vair balls and again,
three other ones in portmanteau dither.

When the meat is served onto a dish or standish

A touch of rot files the degree of leisure under

Sexual difference in addition to head and legs

A better sense of who gave it to her behind

Clumps of trees distinguished by Bad Seeds

The brisure may go elsewhere along disco walls

Elbow grease what crane shot in the sand

Of analysis: valves and onions mirror shelf

Much narrower days alter the familiar

Example of love's ravening flight charged

The breast as if pouncing the existence of an infant

Sudden access to wings or corresponding system

Of tools of which last more anon ruffled by

Our desire for applause the riders list

Angels as common cause for failure they teeter

In the instant crack forward crushing gauntlet

verbal description tempers thicket
of parcel bombs cutaway lure of velours
more starling and correctly argent than a lover's
not resting on spoken language base. Windflowers
call attention to night's vacant signs, how they hint
at booby-trap venus, greater need against heat.
Someone's goodbye in native tongue is experienced
as revisionist rootstock, character's little head-
scarf neatly tied under chin. The content inside could be
crimson overlooking an indication of locale, like hilly
purlieus, long since notched in the flank. Orange-peach
ballots slash bed between quotation marks. It is a minor
obstacle shellacked with two or more coats belonging to
one man made bold by frantic enjambments over the repeated
heraldic scene, her nude airs, elongated buttonhole

further petal makes sexfoil

HERALDIC INDEX

Chris Tysh was born and raised in Paris, and studied American Literature at the Sorbonne. Her book-length *Allen Ginsberg* was published by Seghers in the collection "Poètes d'Aujord'hui."

At present, she teaches creative writing and women's studies at Wayne State University in Detroit. Her books include *Secrets of Elegance, Porné* and *In the Name*.